Services For
The Advent Wreath

Based On Lectionary Years A, B, C

Robert Jarboe

CSS Publishing Company, Inc., Lima, Ohio

This book is dedicated
to my very loving wife Bonnie,
whose support encouraged me
to pursue creative ways
of meaningful worship.

Copyright © 1998 by
CSS Publishing Company, Inc.
Lima, Ohio

ISBN 0-7880-1290-8   PRINTED IN U.S.A.

Introduction

The Advent Wreath is becoming more and more a prevalent symbol of the worship service during the Advent Season. Coming from an old Scandinavian yule tradition, the wreath was used to celebrate the coming of light during a time of darkness (when daylight was at its shortest). Even in Germany, as a part of the celebration, the wreath was hung from the ceiling and celebrants danced beneath it. In the sixth century, a period of penance and devotional preparation in the weeks preceding Christmas was added and the Christian church sanctified it by symbolizing the coming of Christ as the Light of the world after 4,000 years of darkness. By the sixteenth century, it became symbolic of the season for the Christian home.

The wreath itself is composed of a circle of evergreen branches. Staying green throughout the year, the evergreen as well as the wreath circle itself symbolized eternal life, and for some, it was the promise of eternal life by Jesus Christ. There are four candles on the wreath, with three being purple and one pink (symbolizing joy on the Third Sunday of Advent). Churches are now changing the color of the candles to royal blue, because purple is the liturgical color for Lent. Some churches use large white candles with purple ribbons on them, and when Christmas Day arrives, the ribbons are changed to red until Epiphany. The most important part of the Advent Wreath is the large white Christ candle which is at the center.

The Season of Advent focuses upon the messianic prophecies, whereas Christmastide commemorates the birth of Christ, and Epiphany focuses upon the Wise Men following the star. The Advent and Christmas seasons are celebrations of the coming of the Light which is Jesus Christ.

The purpose of this collection is to provide an easy resource, based upon the lectionary, for services for the lighting of the Advent Wreath. Pages with full instructions may be copied for the readers as well as the introits for the choir. To be used by any size church, the following options may be considered:

Options For The Readers
1. Couples from the congregation
2. Two representatives from each adult Sunday school class
3. Two representatives from a woman's group, a men's group, a Bible study, and so forth

Options For Use Of The Introit
1. May be used by the choir: SATB or SAT
2. May be used as a solo: soprano line has the melody
3. May be used as a duet:
   Women: sing SA
   Men: sing SA an octave lower
   Man sings the melody, a woman sings the alto
   Women's choir or trio: sing SAT

In preparation, the Advent Wreath should be placed where it can be easily seen by the congregation as well as accessible to the readers. It should be placed so that there is a candle in front with a candle on each side and a candle in the back (with the pink candle, should it be used, as one of the side candles). The front candle is lit on the First Sunday of Advent, then eventually each side candle, and then the back candle on the fourth Sunday. This way, as the candles are melted down, all four flames will be visible on the Fourth Sunday of Advent. A small white candle used to transfer the light from the altar candle to the wreath should be hidden at the back of the wreath, accessible for the reader. The choral introit is sung at the start of the service as the readers come forward, and the introit is sung once again as the readers return to their seats.

The first page of each section shows how the service is to be entered into the worship bulletin. Also a page for each reader is available, with full instructions as to what to do as well as what to say. Just copy it, write their name on it, and give it to them.

May this resource be helpful in your planning for this coming Advent Season.

Grace and peace to you from Jesus Christ.

Robert S. Jarboe

Revised Common Lectionary

Year A	Year B	Year C
First Sunday Of Advent		
Isaiah 2:1-5	Isaiah 64:1-9	Jeremiah 33:14-16
Psalm 122	Psalm 80:1-7, 17-19	Psalm 25:1-10
Romans 13:11-14	1 Corinthians 1:3-9	1 Thessalonians 3:9-13
Matthew 24:36-44	Mark 13:24-37	Luke 21:25-36
Second Sunday Of Advent		
Isaiah 11:1-10	Isaiah 40:1-11	Malachi 3:1-4
Psalm 72:1-7, 18-19	Psalm 85:1-2, 8-13	Luke 1:68-79
Romans 15:4-13	2 Peter 3:8-15a	Philippians 1:3-11
Matthew 3:1-12	Mark 1:1-8	Luke 3:1-6
Third Sunday Of Advent		
Isaiah 35:1-10	Isaiah 61:1-4, 8-11	Zephaniah 3:14-20
Luke 1:47-55	Psalm 126	Isaiah 12:2-6
James 5:7-10	1 Thessalonians 5:16-24	Philippians 4:4-7
Matthew 11:2-11	John 1:6-8, 19-28	Luke 3:7-18
Fourth Sunday Of Advent		
Isaiah 7:10-16	2 Samuel 7:1-11, 16	Micah 5:2-5a
Psalm 80:1-7, 17-19	Luke 1:47-55	Luke 1:47-55
Romans 1:1-7	Romans 16:25-27	Hebrews 10:5-10
Matthew 1:18-25	Luke 1:26-36	Luke 1:39-45

Christmas Eve
(A, B, and C)
Isaiah 9:2-7
Psalm 96
Titus 2:11-14
Luke 2:1-10

Christmas Day
(A, B, and C)
Isaiah 52:7-10
Psalm 98
Hebrews 1:1-4 (5-12)
John 1:1-14

Bulletin Inserts For Year A

(R - Reader; P - People)

First Sunday Of Advent

Service Of The Advent Wreath   Reader: _____
 Choral Introit
 Litany   Psalm 122:1, 2, 4
 R: Rejoice with me and say with me,
 P: "Let us go into the house of the Lord."
 R: We are standing on holy ground
 P: For this is where we praise God.
 Scripture   Isaiah 2:1-5
 Lighting Of The First Advent Candle
 Prayer
 Choral Introit

Second Sunday Of Advent

Service Of The Advent Wreath   Reader: _____
 Choral Introit
 Litany   Psalm 72:18-19
 R: Praise be to our God!
 P: For our Lord has done marvelous things!
 R: Praise be to God's glorious name forever!
 P: May the whole earth be filled with God's glory.
 Scripture   Isaiah 11:1-10
 Lighting Of The First And Second Advent Candles
 Prayer
 Choral Introit

Third Sunday Of Advent

Service Of The Advent Wreath   Reader: _____
 Choral Introit
 Litany   Isaiah 35:2, 4
 R: Rejoice greatly! Shout for joy!
 P: For we will see the glory of the Lord.
 R: Be strong and do not fear.
 P: For God will come to save us.
 Scripture   Luke 1:47-55
 Lighting Of The First, Second, And Third Advent Candles
 Prayer
 Choral Introit

Fourth Sunday Of Advent

Service Of The Advent Wreath   Reader: _____
  Choral Introit
  Litany   Psalm 80:17-19
  R: Let us call upon the name of the Lord.
  P: Restore us, O Lord God Almighty.
  R: May God's face shine upon us,
  P: That we may be saved.
  Scripture   Isaiah 7:10-16
  Lighting Of The Four Advent Candles
  Prayer
  Choral Introit

Christmas Eve

Service Of The Advent Wreath   Reader: _____
  Choral Introit
  Litany   Psalm 96:12
  R: Sing to the Lord a new song;
      Sing to the Lord all the earth.
  P: Sing to the Lord and praise the Lord's name;
      Proclaim God's salvation day after day.
  Scripture   Isaiah 9:2-7
  Lighting Of The Christ Candle
  Prayer
  Choral Introit

Christmas Day

Service Of The Advent Wreath   Reader: _____
  Choral Introit
  Litany   Isaiah 52:9, 10
  R: Burst into songs of joy!
  P: God has comforted and redeemed us.
  R: In sight of everyone on earth
  P: We shall see the salvation of our God.
  Scripture   John 1:1-14
  Lighting Of The Advent Wreath
  Prayer
  Choral Introit

Words Of Introits For Year A

First Sunday Of Advent
Isaiah 2:1-5 NIV
Light one candle. May the season start as decreed in the last days.
Zion's laws dwell within every heart so that we may know God's ways.
Let us beat swords into plowshares. Let us cause all wars to cease.
Light one candle. Let it brightly burn. O Lord, may we find your peace.

Second Sunday Of Advent
Isaiah 11:1-10 NIV
Light two candles; ever burning bright. Jesse's branch with fruit will show.
For the Spirit of the Lord will light upon all of those who know.
Wolf and lamb will live together. And together they will feed.
Light two candles. Let them brightly burn. And a little child will lead.

Third Sunday Of Advent
Luke 1:47-55 CEV
Light three candles. May they ever glow. All the humble sing aloud.
There is mercy for all those who know. And God scatters all the proud.
God gives good things to the hungry. But the rich are sent away.
Light three candles. Let them brightly burn. O Lord Jesus, come today.

Fourth Sunday Of Advent
Isaiah 7:10-16 NIV
Light four candles. May they ever glow. Prophets said to Israel,
"For a virgin will birth us a son to be named 'Immanuel,'
He is from the house of David knowing wrong, but choosing right."
Light four candles. Let them brightly burn for the Son is God's delight.

Christmas Eve
Isaiah 9:2-7 NIV
Light the candle as we celebrate the Isaiahan prophecy,
"For a child born to us all is giv'n." Angels sing out joyfully.
"He's the Everlasting Father, Mighty God, and Prince of Peace."
Light the candle. Let it brightly burn. "And his reign will never cease."

Christmas Day
John 1:1-14 NIV
Light the candles as we all believe, "The beginning was the Word.
For the Light shines in the darkness, but the light's not understood."
We have seen God's glory through him in the flesh by witnesses.
Light the candles. Let them brightly burn as his glory we confess.

Year A — First Sunday Of Advent

(Distribute this sheet to the readers.)

Date: _____

Reader A: _____   Reader B: _____

Choral Introit
(While the choral introit is being sung, Readers A and B come forward and stand beside the Advent Wreath. Reader B should bring a Bible.)

Litany
Reader A: Please turn to the Advent litany in your bulletins:
                (Pause until the congregation is ready)
                Rejoice with me and say with me,
                "Let us go into the house of the Lord."
                We are standing on holy ground
                For this is where we praise God.

Scripture
Reader B: Our scripture for this First Sunday of Advent is taken from the book of Isaiah, the second chapter, verses one through five.
                (Read Isaiah 2:1-5, preferably the New International Version)

Lighting Of The First Advent Candle
Reader A: As we light the first Advent candle, we do it in the spirit of peace.
(While Reader A is speaking, Reader B takes the small candle hidden in the back of the wreath and transfers the light from the altar candle to the front candle on the Advent Wreath. Then the small candle is placed in back of the wreath.)

Prayer
Reader B: Let us pray: *(pause)* O God, as we enter into this season of Advent, may we exemplify your peace in this world. Help us to walk in your light. Amen.

Choral Introit
(While the choral introit is being sung again, the readers may be seated.)

Note: Should one of the readers be unable to read, let one do the reading while the other transfers the light.

Year A — First Sunday
Isaiah 2:1-5 NIV

R.S.J.

Robert S. Jarboe

Year A — Second Sunday Of Advent

(Distribute this sheet to the readers.)

Date: _____

Reader A: _____   Reader B: _____

Choral Introit
(While the choral introit is being sung, Readers A and B come forward and stand beside the Advent Wreath. Reader B should bring a Bible.)

Litany
Reader A: Please turn to the Advent litany in your bulletins:
(Pause until the congregation is ready)
Praise be to our God!
For our Lord has done marvelous things!
Praise be to God's glorious name forever!
May the whole earth be filled with God's glory.

Scripture
Reader B: Our scripture for this Second Sunday of Advent is taken from the book of Isaiah, the eleventh chapter, verses one through ten.
(Read Isaiah 11:1-10, preferably the New International Version)

Lighting Of The First And Second Advent Candles
Reader A: As we light the first Advent candle, we remember that we are called to a spirit of peace, and as we light the second candle, we do so with a spirit of hope.
(While Reader A is speaking, Reader B takes the small candle hidden in the back of the wreath and transfers the light from the altar candle to the front candle on the Advent Wreath and then to one of the side candles. Then the small candle is placed in back of the wreath.)

Prayer
Reader B: Let us pray: *(pause)* O God, as we are called to be peacemakers, may we respond in hope for that day in which we do not have to live in fear but your justice. Amen.

Choral Introit
(While the choral introit is being sung again, the readers may be seated.)

Note: Should one of the readers be unable to read, let one do the reading while the other transfers the light.

Year A — Second Sunday
Isaiah 11:1-10 NIV

R.S.J.

Robert S. Jarboe

Year A — Third Sunday Of Advent

(Distribute this sheet to the readers.)

Date: _____

Reader A: _____   Reader B: _____

Choral Introit
(While the choral introit is being sung, Readers A and B come forward and stand beside the Advent Wreath. Reader B should bring a Bible.)

Litany
Reader A: Please turn to the Advent litany in your bulletins:
(Pause until the congregation is ready)
Rejoice greatly! Shout for joy!
For we will see the glory of the Lord.
Be strong and do not fear.
For God will come to save us.

Scripture
Reader B: Our scripture for this Third Sunday of Advent is taken from the Gospel of Luke, the first chapter, verses 47 through 55.
(Read Luke 1:47-55, preferably the Contemporary English Version)

Lighting Of The First, Second, And Third Advent Candles
Reader A: As we come to light the Advent Wreath, we recall: The first candle reminds us to live the spirit of peace ... The second candle reminds us to be hopeful ... And now the third candle calls us to joy, for God *will* come to save us.
(While Reader A is speaking, Reader B takes the small candle hidden in the back of the wreath and transfers the light from the altar candle to the front candle on the Advent Wreath, then to each of the side candles. Then the small candle is placed in back of the wreath.)

Prayer
Reader B: Let us pray: *(pause)* O God, this is truly a season of joy, for You have come to us through your Son, Jesus Christ. May there always be praise on our lips and joy in our hearts as we look forward to your coming again. Amen.

Choral Introit
(While the choral introit is being sung again, the readers may be seated.)

Note: Should one of the readers be unable to read, let one do the reading while the other transfers the light.

Year A — Third Sunday
Luke 1:47-55 CEV

R.S.J.

Robert S. Jarboe

15

Year A — Fourth Sunday Of Advent

(Distribute this sheet to the readers.)

Date: _____

Reader A: _____   Reader B: _____

Choral Introit
(While the choral introit is being sung, Readers A and B come forward and stand beside the Advent Wreath. Reader B should bring a Bible.)

Litany
Reader A: Please turn to the Advent litany in your bulletins:
                   (Pause until the congregation is ready)
                   Let us call upon the name of the Lord.
                   Restore us, O Lord God Almighty.
                   May God's face shine upon us,
                   That we may be saved.

Scripture
Reader B: Our scripture for this Fourth Sunday of Advent is taken from the book of Isaiah, the seventh chapter, verses ten through sixteen.
                   (Read Isaiah 7:10-16, preferably the New International Version)

Lighting Of The Four Advent Candles
Reader A: Once again we come to this Advent Wreath. The first candle reminds us to be peaceful. The second candle reminds us to be hopeful. The third candle reminds us to be joyful. And now the fourth candle reminds us to be faithful as God is always faithful to us.
(While Reader A is speaking, Reader B takes the small candle hidden in the back of the wreath and transfers the light from the altar candle to the front candle on the Advent Wreath, then to each of the side candles, and finally to the back candle. Then the small candle is placed in back of the wreath.)

Prayer
Reader B: Let us pray: *(pause)* O God, You call all of us to be faithful; not just knowing right and wrong and choosing right as prophesied about your Son, but to have a deep, abiding faith in You as well. O God, help us to be faithful. Amen.

Choral Introit
(While the choral introit is being sung again, the readers may be seated.)

Note: Should one of the readers be unable to read, let one do the reading while the other transfers the light.

Year A— Fourth Sunday
Isaiah 7:10-16 NIV

R.S.J.

Robert S. Jarboe

Piano Intro. (Choir:) Light four can-dles. May they ev-er glow. Pro-phets said to Is-ra-el, "For a vir-gin will birth us a son to be named Im-ma-nu-el. He is from the house of Da-vid know-ing wrong, but choos-ing right." Light four can-dles. Let them bright-ly burn for the Son is God's de-light.

Year A — Christmas Eve

(Distribute this sheet to the readers.)

Date: _____

Reader A: _____   Reader B: _____

Choral Introit
(While the choral introit is being sung, Readers A and B come forward and stand beside the Advent Wreath. Reader B should bring a Bible.)

Litany
Reader A: Please turn to the Advent litany in your bulletins:
            (Pause until the congregation is ready)
            Sing to the Lord a new song;
            Sing to the Lord all the earth.
            Sing to the Lord and praise the Lord's name;
            Proclaim God's salvation day after day.

Scripture
Reader B: Our scripture for this Christmas Eve is taken from the book of Isaiah, the ninth chapter, verses two through seven.
            (Read Isaiah 9:2-7, preferably the New International Version)

Lighting Of The Christ Candle
Reader A: On this holy night, we light only the Christ candle. As we have been called to be peaceful, hopeful, joyful, and faithful, let us now proclaim Christ as the Light of the world.
*(While Reader A is speaking, Reader B takes the small candle hidden in the back of the wreath and transfers the light from the altar candle to the Christ candle at the center of the wreath. **Do not light the four Advent candles.** Then the small candle is placed in back of the wreath.)*

Prayer
Reader B: Let us pray: *(pause)* O God, You call all of us to be faithful; not just knowing right and wrong and choosing right as prophesied about your Son, but to have a deep, abiding faith in You as well. O God, help us to be faithful. Amen.

Choral Introit
(While the choral introit is being sung again, the readers may be seated.)

Note: Should one of the readers be unable to read, let one do the reading while the other transfers the light.

Year A — Christmas Eve
Isaiah 9:2-7 NIV

R.S.J.

Robert S. Jarboe

Piano Intro. (Choir:) Light the can - dle as we ce - le -brate the Is - aia - han pro - phe - cy. "For a child born to us all is giv'n." An - gels sing out joy - ful - ly. "He's the e - ver - last - ing Fa - ther, Migh ty God and Prince of Peace." Light the can - dle. Let it bright ly burn. "And his reign will ne - ver cease."

Year A — Christmas Day

(Distribute this sheet to the readers.)

Date: _____

Reader A: _____   Reader B: _____

Choral Introit
(While the choral introit is being sung, Readers A and B come forward and stand beside the Advent Wreath. Reader B should bring a Bible.)

Litany
Reader A: Please turn to the Advent litany in your bulletins:
            (Pause until the congregation is ready)
            Burst into songs of joy!
            God has comforted and redeemed us.
            In sight of everyone on earth
            We shall see the salvation of our God.

Scripture
Reader B: Our scripture for this Christmas Day is taken from the Gospel of John, chapter one, verses one through fourteen.
            (Read John 1:1-14, preferably the New International Version)

Lighting Of The Advent Wreath
Reader A: As we relight the Christ candle as well as the candles of peace, hope, joy, and faith, may we remember that Christ comes as the Light that shines in the darkness.
(While Reader A is speaking, Reader B takes the small candle hidden in the back of the wreath and transfers the light from the altar candle to first the Christ candle in the center of the wreath and then to the four surrounding candles. Then the small candle is placed in back of the wreath.)

Prayer
Reader B: Let us pray: *(pause)* O God, as we celebrate this day of your Son's coming on Earth, may we truly sing with joy, for Christ is the true salvation of God. Amen.

Choral Introit
(While the choral introit is being sung again, the readers may be seated.)

Note: Should one of the readers be unable to read, let one do the reading while the other transfers the light.

Year A — Christmas Day
John 1:1-14 NIV

R.S.J.

Robert S. Jarboe

Bulletin Inserts For Year B

(R - Reader; P - People)

First Sunday Of Advent

Service Of The Advent Wreath   Reader: _____
  Choral Introit
  Litany   Psalm 80:17-19
  R: Let us call upon the name of the Lord.
  P: Restore us, O Lord God Almighty.
  R: May God's face shine upon us,
  P: That we may be saved.
  Scripture   Isaiah 64:1-9
  Lighting Of The First Advent Candle
  Prayer
  Choral Introit

Second Sunday Of Advent

Service Of The Advent Wreath   Reader: _____
  Choral Introit
  Litany   Psalm 85:11, 13
  R: Let faithfulness spring forth from the earth,
  P: And righteousness look down from heaven.
  R: The Lord gives what is good.
  P: Therefore, let us prepare the Lord's way.
  Scripture   Isaiah 40:1-11
  Lighting Of The First And Second Advent Candles
  Prayer
  Choral Introit

Third Sunday Of Advent

Service Of The Advent Wreath   Reader: _____
  Choral Introit
  Litany   Psalm 126:2, 5, 6
  R: The Lord has done great things for us, and we are filled with joy.
  P: Those who sow in tears will reap with songs of joy.
  R: Whoever goes out weeping, carrying seeds to sow,
  P: Will return with songs of joy.
  Scripture   Isaiah 61:1-4, 8-11
  Lighting Of The First, Second, And Third Advent Candles
  Prayer
  Choral Introit

Fourth Sunday Of Advent

Service Of The Advent Wreath   Reader: _____

Choral Introit

Litany   Luke 1:46-47

R: With all our hearts

P: We praise the Lord.

R: And we are glad

P: Because of God our Savior.

Scripture   Luke 1:47-55

Lighting Of The Four Advent Candles

Prayer

Choral Introit

Christmas Eve

Service Of The Advent Wreath   Reader: _____

Choral Introit

Litany   Psalm 96:12

R: Sing to the Lord a new song;
   Sing to the Lord all the earth.

P: Sing to the Lord and praise the Lord's name;
   Proclaim God's salvation day after day.

Scripture   Isaiah 9:2-7

Lighting Of The Christ Candle

Prayer

Choral Introit

Christmas Day

Service Of The Advent Wreath   Reader: _____

Choral Introit

Litany   Isaiah 52:9, 10

R: Burst into songs of joy!

P: God has comforted and redeemed us.

R: In sight of everyone on earth

P: We shall see the salvation of our God.

Scripture   John 1:1-14

Lighting Of The Advent Wreath

Prayer

Choral Introit

Words Of Introits For Year B

First Sunday Of Advent
Isaiah 64:1-9 CEV
Light one candle. May this season start with a hope that starts to burn
A desire within ev'ry heart calling for your soon return.
All our sins are like the storm winds; we like leaves are swept away.
Light one candle. Let it brightly burn. May You come to us today.

Second Sunday Of Advent
Isaiah 40:1-11 CEV
Light two candles. May they ever glow while our faith calls us to wait.
There's a shouting, "Make each mountain low and the desert road make straight."
Lord, we know You're never changing. Make our paths; show us the way.
Light two candles. Let them brightly burn. Kindle, Lord, our faith today.

Third Sunday Of Advent
Isaiah 61:1-4, 8-11 CEV
Light three candles. May they ever glow. May your Good News calm our fears.
Give us flowers and not sorrow, olive oil in place of tears.
Lord, You heal the brokenhearted. We are captive, give release.
Light three candles. Let them brightly burn. May our joy in You increase.

Fourth Sunday Of Advent
Luke 1:47-55 CEV
Light four candles. May they ever glow. All the humble sing aloud.
There is mercy for all those who know. And God scatters all the proud.
God gives good things to the hungry. But the rich are sent away.
Light four candles. Let them brightly burn. O Lord Jesus, come today.

Christmas Eve
Isaiah 9:2-7 NIV
Light the candle as we celebrate the Isaiahan prophecy,
"For a child born to us all is giv'n." Angels sing out joyfully.
"He's the Everlasting Father, Mighty God, and Prince of Peace."
Light the candle. Let it brightly burn. "And his reign will never cease."

Christmas Day
John 1:1-14 NIV
Light the candles as we all believe, "The beginning was the Word.
For the Light shines in the darkness, but the light's not understood."
We have seen God's glory through him in the flesh by witnesses.
Light the candles. Let them brightly burn as his glory we confess.

Year B — First Sunday Of Advent

(Distribute this sheet to the readers.)

Date: _____

Reader A: _____   Reader B: _____

Choral Introit
(While the choral introit is being sung, Readers A and B come forward and stand beside the Advent Wreath. Reader B should bring a Bible.)

Litany
Reader A: Please turn to the Advent litany in your bulletins:
            (Pause until the congregation is ready)
            Let us call upon the name of the Lord.
            Restore us, O Lord God Almighty.
            May God's face shine upon us,
            That we may be saved.

Scripture
Reader B: Our scripture for this First Sunday of Advent is taken from the book of Isaiah, the sixty-fourth chapter, verses one through nine.
            (Read Isaiah 64:1-9, preferably the Contemporary English Version)

Lighting Of The First Advent Candle
Reader A: As we light the first Advent candle with the hope and the desire for the coming of the Lord.
(While Reader A is speaking, Reader B takes the small candle hidden in the back of the wreath and transfers the light from the altar candle to the front candle on the Advent Wreath. Then the small candle is placed in back of the wreath.)

Prayer
Reader B: Let us pray: *(pause)* O God, it seems that the sins of the world are so overwhelming that we feel hopeless. Reignite our faith so that our hope would truly be in You, for You are our only salvation. Amen.

Choral Introit
(While the choral introit is being sung again, the readers may be seated.)

Note: Should one of the readers be unable to read, let one do the reading while the other transfers the light.

Year B — First Sunday
Isaiah 64:1-9 CEV

R.S.J.

Robert S. Jarboe

Piano Intro. (Choir:) Light one can - dle. May this

sea-son start with a hope that starts to burn. a de - sire - - with in

ev -'ry heart call-ing for your soon re - turn. All our sins are like the

storm winds; we like leaves are swept a - way - -Light one can - dle. Let it

bright-ly burn. May You come to us to - day.

(c)1996 R.S. Jarboe

27

Year B — Second Sunday Of Advent

(Distribute this sheet to the readers.)

Date: _____

Reader A: _____   Reader B: _____

Choral Introit
(While the choral introit is being sung, Readers A and B come forward and stand beside the Advent Wreath. Reader B should bring a Bible.)

Litany
Reader A: Please turn to the Advent litany in your bulletins:
(Pause until the congregation is ready)
Let faithfulness spring forth from the earth,
And righteousness look down from heaven.
The Lord gives what is good.
Therefore, let us prepare the Lord's way.

Scripture
Reader B: Our scripture for this Second Sunday of Advent is taken from the book of Isaiah, the fortieth chapter, verses one through eleven.
(Read Isaiah 40:1-11, preferably the Contemporary English Version)

Lighting Of The First And Second Advent Candles
Reader A: The first Advent candle is lighted again with hope, and we light the second candle calling us to a faith that God's Kingdom will come.
(While Reader A is speaking, Reader B takes the small candle hidden in the back of the wreath and transfers the light from the altar candle to the front candle on the Advent Wreath and then one of the side candles. Then the small candle is placed in back of the wreath.)

Prayer
Reader B: Let us pray: *(pause)* O God, we know that You are ever faithful. Help us to be faithful to You in word and deed so that we may be worthy for the coming of your Kingdom. Amen.

Choral Introit
(While the choral introit is being sung again, the readers may be seated.)

Note: Should one of the readers be unable to read, let one do the reading while the other transfers the light.

Year B — Second Sunday
Isaiah 40:1-11 CEV

R.S.J.

Robert S. Jarboe

Piano Intro. (Choir:) Light two can-dles. May they e-ver glow while our faith calls us to wait. There's a shout-ing, "Make each moun-tain low and the de-sert road make straight." Lord, we know you're ne-ver chang-ing. Make our paths; show us the way. Light two can-dles. Let them bright ly burn. Kin-dle, Lord, our faith to - day.

Year B — Third Sunday Of Advent

(Distribute this sheet to the readers.)

Date: _____

Reader A: _____   Reader B: _____

Choral Introit
(While the choral introit is being sung, Readers A and B come forward and stand beside the Advent Wreath. Reader B should bring a Bible.)

Litany
Reader A: Please turn to the Advent litany in your bulletins:
(Pause until the congregation is ready)
The Lord has done great things for us, and we are filled with joy.
Those who sow in tears will reap with songs of joy.
Whoever goes out weeping, carrying seeds to sow,
Will return with songs of joy.

Scripture
Reader B: Our scripture for this Third Sunday of Advent is taken from the book of Isaiah, the sixty-first chapter, verses one through four and eight through eleven.
(Read Isaiah 61:1-4, 8-11, preferably the Contemporary English Version)

Lighting Of The First, Second, And Third Advent Candles
Reader A: As we light the candles of hope and faith, we add the candle of joy. The Good News is that the broken-hearted will be healed and those who are held captive will be set free.
(While Reader A is speaking, Reader B takes the small candle hidden in the back of the wreath and transfers the light from the altar candle to the front candle on the Advent Wreath and then to the side candles. Then the small candle is placed in back of the wreath.)

Prayer
Reader B: Let us pray: *(pause)* O God, we know that You have done great things for our good. Help us to experience your joy in our sorrow so that our broken hearts may be healed through your son. Amen.

Choral Introit
(While the choral introit is being sung again, the readers may be seated.)

Note: Should one of the readers be unable to read, let one do the reading while the other transfers the light.

Year B — Third Sunday
Isaiah 61:1-4, 8-11 CEV

R.S.J.

Robert S. Jarboe

Piano Intro. (Choir:) Light three can - dles. May they

e - ver glow. May your Good News calm our fears. Give us flo - wers and not

sor - row, o - live oil in place of tears. Lord, You heal the bro - ken -

heart - ed. We are cap - tive, give re - lease. Light three can - dles. Let them

bright ly burn. May our joy in You in - crease.

Year B — Fourth Sunday Of Advent

(Distribute this sheet to the readers.)

Date: _____

Reader A: _____   Reader B: _____

Choral Introit
(While the choral introit is being sung, Readers A and B come forward and stand beside the Advent Wreath. Reader B should bring a Bible.)

Litany
Reader A: Please turn to the Advent litany in your bulletins:
             (Pause until the congregation is ready)
             With all our hearts
             We praise the Lord.
             And we are glad
             Because of God our Savior.

Scripture
Reader B: Our scripture for this Fourth Sunday of Advent is taken from the Gospel of Luke, the first chapter, verses 47 through 55.
             (Read Luke 1:47-55, preferably the Contemporary English Version)

Lighting Of The Four Advent Candles
Reader A: Once again we come to this Advent Wreath. The first candle reminds us to be hopeful. The second candle reminds us to be faithful. The third candle reminds us to be joyful. And now we light the fourth candle symbolizing peace, because our all-powerful God is merciful and cares for the humble.
(While Reader A is speaking, Reader B takes the small candle hidden in the back of the wreath and transfers the light from the altar candle to the front candle on the Advent Wreath, then to each of the side candles, and finally to the back candle. Then the small candle is placed in back of the wreath.)

Prayer
Reader B: Let us pray: *(pause)* O God, we give You praise and glory for the everlasting life that You bring through your Son. For You have brought down those who thought they were powerful and You have raised up the humble of heart. Amen.

Choral Introit
(While the choral introit is being sung again, the readers may be seated.)

Note: Should one of the readers be unable to read, let one do the reading while the other transfers the light.

Year B — Fourth Sunday
Luke 1:47-55 CEV

R.S.J.

Robert S. Jarboe

Year B — Christmas Eve

(Distribute this sheet to the readers.)

Date: _____

Reader A: _____ Reader B: _____

Choral Introit
(While the choral introit is being sung, Readers A and B come forward and stand beside the Advent Wreath. Reader B should bring a Bible.)

Litany
Reader A: Please turn to the Advent litany in your bulletins:
   (Pause until the congregation is ready)
   Sing to the Lord a new song;
   Sing to the Lord all the earth.
   Sing to the Lord and praise the Lord's name;
   Proclaim God's salvation day after day.

Scripture
Reader B: Our scripture for this Christmas Eve is taken from the book of Isaiah, the ninth chapter, verses two through seven.
   (Read Isaiah 9:2-7, preferably the New International Version)

Lighting Of The Christ Candle
Reader A: On this holy night, we light only the Christ candle. As we have been called to be peaceful, hopeful, joyful, and faithful, let us now proclaim Christ as the Light of the world.
*(While Reader A is speaking, Reader B takes the small candle hidden in the back of the wreath and transfers the light from the altar candle to the Christ candle at the center of the wreath. **Do not light the four Advent candles.** Then the small candle is placed in back of the wreath.)*

Prayer
Reader B: Let us pray: *(pause)* O God, You call all of us to be faithful; not just knowing right and wrong and choosing right as prophesied about your Son, but to have a deep, abiding faith in You as well. O God, help us to be faithful. Amen.

Choral Introit
(While the choral introit is being sung again, the readers may be seated.)

Note: Should one of the readers be unable to read, let one do the reading while the other transfers the light.

Year B — Christmas Eve
Isaiah 9:2-7 NIV

R.S.J.

Robert S. Jarboe

(c)1996 R.S. Jarboe

35

Year B — Christmas Day

(Distribute this sheet to the readers.)

Date: _____

Reader A: _____   Reader B: _____

Choral Introit
(While the choral introit is being sung, Readers A and B come forward and stand beside the Advent Wreath. Reader B should bring a Bible.)

Litany
Reader A: Please turn to the Advent litany in your bulletins:
  (Pause until the congregation is ready)
  Burst into songs of joy!
  God has comforted and redeemed us.
  In sight of everyone on earth
  We shall see the salvation of our God.

Scripture
Reader B: Our scripture for this Christmas Day is taken from the Gospel of John, chapter one, verses one through fourteen.
  (Read John 1:1-14, preferably the New International Version)

Lighting Of The Advent Wreath
Reader A: As we relight the Christ Candle as well as the candles of peace, hope, joy, and faith, may we remember that Christ comes as the Light that shines in the darkness.
(While Reader A is speaking, Reader B takes the small candle hidden in the back of the wreath and transfers the light from the altar candle to first the Christ Candle at the center of the wreath and then to the four surrounding candles. Then the small candle is placed in back of the wreath.)

Prayer
Reader B: Let us pray: *(pause)* O God, as we celebrate this day of your Son's coming on Earth, may we truly sing with joy, for Christ is the true salvation of God. Amen.

Choral Introit
(While the choral introit is being sung again, the readers may be seated.)

Note: Should one of the readers be unable to read, let one do the reading while the other transfers the light.

Year B — Christmas Day
John 1:1-14 NIC

R.S.J.

Robert S. Jarboe

Piano Intro.

(Choir:) Light the can - dles as we all be - lieve "The be - gin - ning was the Word. For the light shines in the dark - ness, but the light's not un - der - stood." We have seen God's glo - ry through Him in the flesh by wit - ness - es. Light the can - dles. Let them bright ly burn as his glo - ry we con - fess.

Bulletin Inserts For Year C

(R - Reader; P - People)

First Sunday Of Advent

Service Of The Advent Wreath
    Choral Introit
    Litany
    R: To you, O Lord, we lift up our souls.
    P: We trust in you, O God.
    R: All God's ways are loving and faithful
    P: To those who keep the covenant.
    Scripture
    Lighting Of The First Advent Candle
    Prayer
    Choral Introit

Reader: _____

Psalm 25:1, 2, 10

Jeremiah 33:14-16

Second Sunday Of Advent

Service Of The Advent Wreath
    Choral Introit
    Litany
    R: Praise be to God!
    P: Who has come and brought redemption.
    R: As prophesied long ago,
    P: God's salvation will strengthen us and show us the way to peace.
    Scripture
    Lighting Of The First And Second Advent Candles
    Prayer
    Choral Introit

Reader: _____

Luke 1:68, 70, 74, 79

Malachi 3:1-4

Third Sunday Of Advent

Service Of The Advent Wreath
    Choral Introit
    Litany
    R: The Lord is our strength, our song, and our salvation.
    P: And with joy we will see the salvation of the Lord.
    R: Shout aloud and sing for joy!
    P: For great is the God of Israel.
    Scripture
    Lighting Of The First, Second, And Third Advent Candles
    Prayer
    Choral Introit

Reader: _____

Isaiah 12:2, 3, 6

Zephaniah 3:14-20

Fourth Sunday Of Advent

Service Of The Advent Wreath   Reader: _____
    Choral Introit
    Litany   Micah 5:4
    R: Jesus is our Lord and our Shepherd,
    P: And in him we find strength.
    R: When he comes, we will be secure,
    P: And his greatness will reach the ends of the earth.
    Scripture   Luke 1:47-55
    Lighting Of The Four Advent Candles
    Prayer
    Choral Introit

Christmas Eve

Service Of The Advent Wreath   Reader: _____
    Choral Introit
    Litany   Psalm 96:12
    R: Sing to the Lord a new song;
        Sing to the Lord all the earth.
    P: Sing to the Lord and praise the Lord's name;
        Proclaim God's salvation day after day.
    Scripture   Isaiah 9:2-7
    Lighting Of The Christ Candle
    Prayer
    Choral Introit

Christmas Day

Service Of The Advent Wreath   Reader: _____
    Choral Introit
    Litany   Isaiah 52:9, 10
    R: Burst into songs of joy!
    P: God has comforted and redeemed us.
    R: In sight of everyone on earth
    P: We shall see the salvation of our God.
    Scripture   John 1:1-14
    Lighting Of The Advent Wreath
    Prayer
    Choral Introit

Words Of Introits For Year C

First Sunday Of Advent
Jeremiah 33:14-16 NIV

Light one candle. May this season start. "Days are coming," says the Lord.
There's a promise held in Israel's heart shared by Jeremiah's word.
"I will make a righteous branch sprout up from the Davidic line."
Light one candle. May it brightly burn. May the Lord our Righteous shine.

Second Sunday Of Advent
Malachi 3:1-4 NIV

Light two candles. May they ever glow. For the one prepares the way
With a message of the Covenant, but who can endure that day?
Who can stand the Lord's appearing coming as refining fire?
Light two candles. Let them brightly burn filling our holy desire.

Third Sunday Of Advent
Zephaniah 3:14-20 CEV

Light three candles. May they ever glow. We will shout and celebrate.
For the troubles and the punishments our Lord will one day abate.
For the Lord, the King of Israel, in his love will lead us home.
Light three candles. Let them brightly burn. We will see God's blessings come.

Fourth Sunday Of Advent
Luke 1:47-55 CEV

Light four candles. May they ever glow. All the humble sing aloud.
There is mercy for all those who know. And God scatters all the proud.
God gives good things to the hungry. But the rich are sent away.
Light four candles. Let them brightly burn. O Lord Jesus, come today.

Christmas Eve
Isaiah 9:2-7 NIV

Light the candle as we celebrate the Isaiahan prophecy,
"For a child born to us all is giv'n." Angels sing out joyfully.
"He's the Everlasting Father, Mighty God, and Prince of Peace."
Light the candle. Let it brightly burn. "And his reign will never cease."

Christmas Day
John 1:1-14 NIV

Light the candles as we all believe, "The beginning was the Word.
For the Light shines in the darkness, but the light's not understood."
We have seen God's glory through him in the flesh by witnesses.
Light the candles. Let them brightly burn as his glory we confess.

Year C — First Sunday Of Advent

(Distribute this sheet to the readers.)

Date: _____

Reader A: _____   Reader B: _____

Choral Introit
(While the choral introit is being sung, Readers A and B come forward and stand beside the Advent Wreath. Reader B should bring a Bible.)

Litany
Reader A: Please turn to the Advent litany in your bulletins:
　　　　　　(Pause until the congregation is ready)
　　　　　　To You, O Lord, we lift up our souls.
　　　　　　We trust in you, O God.
　　　　　　All God's ways are loving and faithful
　　　　　　To those who keep the covenant.

Scripture
Reader B: Our scripture for this First Sunday of Advent is taken from the book of Jeremiah, the thirty-third chapter, verses fourteen through sixteen.
　　　　　　(Read Jeremiah 33:14-16, preferably the New International Version)

Lighting Of The First Advent Candle
Reader A: We light the first candle to remind us of the hope we have in God's promise of the Messianic Kingdom.
(While Reader A is speaking, Reader B takes the small candle hidden in the back of the wreath and transfers the light from the altar candle to the front candle on the Advent Wreath. Then the small candle is placed in back of the wreath.)

Prayer
Reader B: Let us pray: *(pause)* O God, Our only true hope is in You. We trust your promises for us that your great Kingdom will come. Amen.

Choral Introit
(While the choral introit is being sung again, the readers may be seated.)

Note: Should one of the readers be unable to read, let one do the reading while the other transfers the light.

Year C — First Sunday
Jeremiah 33:14-16 NIV

R.S.J.

Robert S. Jarboe

(c)1996 R.S. Jarboe

Year C — Second Sunday Of Advent

(Distribute this sheet to the readers.)

Date: _____

Reader A: _____   Reader B: _____

Choral Introit
(While the choral introit is being sung, Readers A and B come forward and stand beside the Advent Wreath. Reader B should bring a Bible.)

Litany
Reader A: Please turn to the Advent litany in your bulletins:
            (Pause until the congregation is ready)
            Praise be to God!
            Who has come and brought redemption.
            As prophesied long ago,
            God's salvation will strengthen us and show us the way to peace.

Scripture
Reader B: Our scripture for this Second Sunday of Advent is taken from the book of Malachi, the third chapter, verses one through four.
            (Read Malachi 3:1-4, preferably the New International Version)

Lighting Of The First And Second Advent Candles
Reader A: After lighting the first candle of hope, we light the second candle of peace, reminding us that God will refine and purify us for the Kingdom to come that we may prove acceptable.
(While Reader A is speaking, Reader B takes the small candle hidden in the back of the wreath and transfers the light from the altar candle to the front candle on the Advent Wreath and then one of the side candles. Then the small candle is placed in back of the wreath.)

Prayer
Reader B: Let us pray: *(pause)* O God, as the one who has prepared the way to your coming, help us to prepare for your Kingdom so that we may realize a peace we've never known before. Amen.

Choral Introit
(While the choral introit is being sung again, the readers may be seated.)

Note: Should one of the readers be unable to read, let one do the reading while the other transfers the light.

Year C — Second Sunday
Malachi 3:1-4 NIV

R.S.J.

Robert S. Jarboe

Piano Intro. (Choir:) Light two can-dles. May they e-ver glow. For the one pre-pares the way. - With a mes-sage of the Co-ve-nant, but who can en-dure that day? Who can stand the Lord's ap-pear-ing com-ing as re-fin-ing fire? - Light two can-dles. Let them bright-ly burn fill-ing our ho-ly de-sire.

Year C — Third Sunday Of Advent

(Distribute this sheet to the readers.)

Date: _____

Reader A: _____   Reader B: _____

Choral Introit
(While the choral introit is being sung, Readers A and B come forward and stand beside the Advent Wreath. Reader B should bring a Bible.)

Litany
Reader A: Please turn to the Advent litany in your bulletins:
(Pause until the congregation is ready)
The Lord is our strength, our song, and our salvation.
And with joy we will see the salvation of the Lord.
Shout aloud and sing for joy!
For great is the God of Israel.

Scripture
Reader B: Our scripture for this Third Sunday of Advent is taken from the book of Zephaniah, the third chapter, verses fourteen through twenty.
(Read Zephaniah 3:14-20, preferably the Contemporary English Version)

Lighting Of The First, Second, And Third Advent Candles
Reader A: As we light the candles of hope and peace, we also light the candle of joy, for the prophet Zephaniah calls us to celebrate what God has done and what God will do.
(While Reader A is speaking, Reader B takes the small candle hidden in the back of the wreath and transfers the light from the altar candle to the front candle on the Advent Wreath and then to the side candles. Then the small candle is placed in back of the wreath.)

Prayer
Reader B: Let us pray: *(pause)* O God, we do believe that You are our salvation and our strength. May our joy be complete in You, knowing that You will fulfill your promises. Amen.

Choral Introit
(While the choral introit is being sung again, the readers may be seated.)

Note: Should one of the readers be unable to read, let one do the reading while the other transfers the light.

Year C — Third Sunday
Zephaniah 3:14-20 CEV

R.S.J.

Robert S. Jarboe

Year C — Fourth Sunday Of Advent

(Distribute this sheet to the readers.)

Date: _____

Reader A: _____   Reader B: _____

Choral Introit
(While the choral introit is being sung, Readers A and B come forward and stand beside the Advent Wreath. Reader B should bring a Bible.)

Litany
Reader A: Please turn to the Advent litany in your bulletins:
(Pause until the congregation is ready)
Jesus is our Lord and Shepherd,
And in him we find strength.
When he comes, we will be secure,
And his greatness will reach the ends of the earth.

Scripture
Reader B: Our scripture for this Fourth Sunday of Advent is taken from the Gospel of Luke, the first chapter, verses 47 through 55.
(Read Luke 1:47-55, preferably the Contemporary English Version)

Lighting Of The Four Advent Candles
Reader A: Once again we come to this Advent Wreath. As we light the candles reminding us of hope, peace, and joy, we add the candle of faith. Mary was faithful in her simple understanding of God, and God was faithful in fulfilling the promises to Israel.
(While Reader A is speaking, Reader B takes the small candle hidden in the back of the wreath and transfers the light from the altar candle to the front candle on the Advent Wreath, then to each of the side candles, and finally to the back candle. Then the small candle is placed in back of the wreath.)

Prayer
Reader B: Let us pray: *(pause)* O God, as we realize You have been faithful throughout time, may we be faithful in trust and obedience to You. Amen.

Choral Introit
(While the choral introit is being sung again, the readers may be seated.)

Note: Should one of the readers be unable to read, let one do the reading while the other transfers the light.

Year C — Fourth Sunday
Luke 1:47-55 CEV

R.S.J.

Robert S. Jarboe

Year C — Christmas Eve

(Distribute this sheet to the readers.)

Date: _____

Reader A: _____   Reader B: _____

Choral Introit
(While the choral introit is being sung, Readers A and B come forward and stand beside the Advent Wreath. Reader B should bring a Bible.)

Litany
Reader A: Please turn to the Advent litany in your bulletins:
         (Pause until the congregation is ready)
         Sing to the Lord a new song;
         Sing to the Lord all the earth.
         Sing to the Lord and praise the Lord's name;
         Proclaim God's salvation day after day.

Scripture
Reader B: Our scripture for this Christmas Eve is taken from the book of Isaiah, the ninth chapter, verses two through seven.
         (Read Isaiah 9:2-7, preferably the New International Version)

Lighting Of The Christ Candle
Reader A: On this holy night, we light only the Christ candle. As we have been called to be peaceful, hopeful, joyful, and faithful, let us now proclaim Christ as the Light of the world.
*(While Reader A is speaking, Reader B takes the small candle hidden in the back of the wreath and transfers the light from the altar candle to the Christ candle at the center of the wreath. **Do not light the four Advent candles.** Then the small candle is placed in back of the wreath.)*

Prayer
Reader B: Let us pray: *(pause)* O God, You call all of us to be faithful; not just knowing right and wrong and choosing right as prophesied about your Son, but to have a deep, abiding faith in You as well. O God, help us to be faithful. Amen.

Choral Introit
(While the choral introit is being sung again, the readers may be seated.)

Note: Should one of the readers be unable to read, let one do the reading while the other transfers the light.

Year C — Christmas Eve
Isaiah 9:2-7 NIV

R.S.J.

Robert S. Jarboe

Piano Intro. (Choir:) Light the can - dle as we ce - le brate the Is - aia - han pro - phe - cy, "For a child born to us all is giv'n." An - gels sing out joy - ful - ly. "He's the e - ver - last - ing Fa - ther, Might y God and Prince of Peace." Light the can - dle. Let it bright ly burn. "And his reign will ne - ver cease."

Year C — Christmas Day

(Distribute this sheet to the readers.)

Date: _____

Reader A: _____   Reader B: _____

Choral Introit
(While the choral introit is being sung, Readers A and B come forward and stand beside the Advent Wreath. Reader B should bring a Bible.)

Litany
Reader A: Please turn to the Advent litany in your bulletins:
(Pause until the congregation is ready)
Burst into songs of joy!
God has comforted and redeemed us.
In sight of everyone on earth
We shall see the salvation of our God.

Scripture
Reader B: Our scripture for this Christmas Day is taken from the Gospel of John, chapter one, verses one through fourteen.
(Read John 1:1-14, preferably the New International Version)

Lighting Of The Advent Wreath
Reader A: As we relight the Christ candle as well as the candles of peace, hope, joy, and faith, may we remember that Christ comes as the Light that shines in the darkness.
(While Reader A is speaking, Reader B takes the small candle hidden in the back of the wreath and transfers the light from the altar candle to first the Christ candle at the center of the wreath and then to the four surrounding candles. Then the small candle is placed in back of the wreath.)

Prayer
Reader B: Let us pray: *(pause)* O God, as we celebrate this day of your Son's coming on Earth, may we truly sing with joy, for Christ is the true salvation of God. Amen.

Choral Introit
(While the choral introit is being sung again, the readers may be seated.)

Note: Should one of the readers be unable to read, let one do the reading while the other transfers the light.

Year C — Christmas Day
John 1:1-14 NIV

R.S.J.

Robert S. Jarboe

Who Are You?
8, 6, 8, 6

Robert S. Jarboe

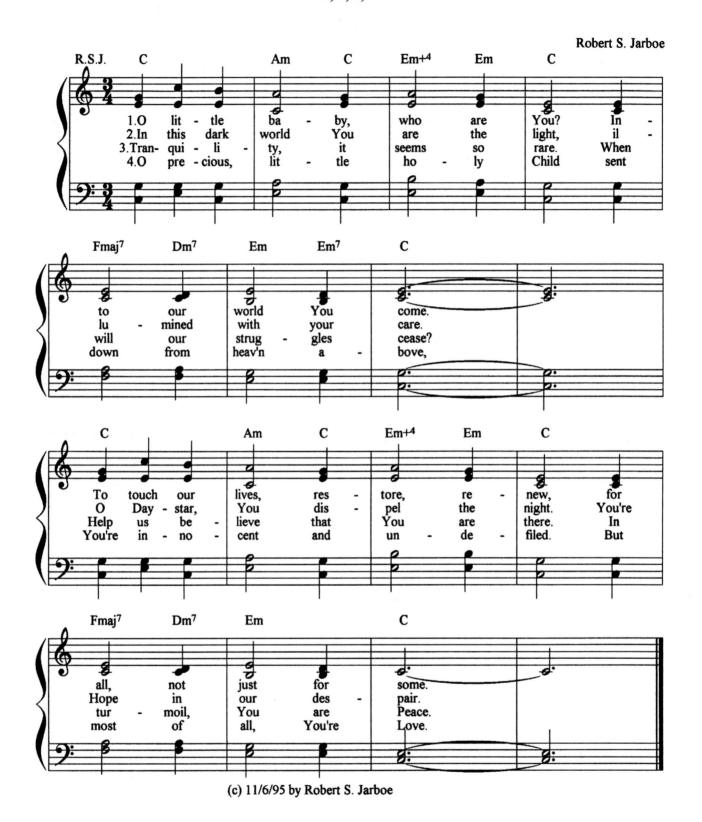

This Child, Emmanuel
8, 6, 8, 6

R.S.J.

Robert S. Jarboe

1. Who is this One - who reigns in hearts; - Of whom the an - gels sing, - Who
2. This in - no - cent - life has be-gun, - As God's Word does re - call, - A
3. No - one can know - or ful- ly claim How God can love so well. - For
4. For God is with- - us thru all time- -And ev - 'ry heart shall see - Em -

thru God's love, God's grace im - parts, This child who is the King?
per - fect life - to be God's Son; This child, the Lord of all.
ge - ner - a - tions give the name, This child, "Em-man - u - el."
man - u - el - our Lord and King, For all e - ter - ni - ty.

Bibliography

Behm, Douglas R., *An Advent Covenant Wreath*, CSS Publishing Company, Lima, Ohio, 1981.

Crippen, T.G., *Christmas And Christmas Lore*, Gale Research Company, Detroit, Michigan, 1971.

Dessem, Ralph, *Celebrating Advent In The Sanctuary*, CSS Publishing Company, Lima, Ohio, 1994.

Liesch, Barry, *People In The Presence Of God*, Zondervan Publishing House, Grand Rapids, Michigan, 1988.

Stevens, Patricia Bunnin, *Merry Christmas! A History Of The Holiday*, Macmillan Publishing Company, New York, 1979.

Webber, Robert, Editor, *The Complete Library Of Christian Worship: Volume Five, Services Of The Christian Year*, Star Song Publishing, Nashville, Tennessee, 1994.

Webber, Robert, *Worship Is A Verb*, Abbott Martyn, Nashville, Tennessee, 1992.